CB129883

Cambridge Little Steps 3

Student's Book

Gabriela Zapiain

CAMBRIDGE
UNIVERSITY PRESS

Cambridge Little Steps 3

1 What do we do at school?

Listen. Say. Sing.

Monday

Tuesday

Wednesday

Thursday

Friday

Saturday and Sunday

Key Vocabulary: *Monday, Tuesday, Wednesday, Thursday, Friday, Saturday, Sunday*

Tracks: 1 and 2

What is the story about?

Listen. Point. Say.

We Learn at School!

hat

coat

bee

On Monday, we learn to be tidy and neat.
I hang up my hat.
I put my coat next to that.
And I take my shoes with mud off my feet.

On Tuesday and Wednesday, we learn how to color things.
I use green for the trees. I use yellow and black for the bees.
And I use blue for the beautiful butterfly wings.

Key Vocabulary: *hat, coat, bee, tree, wing, thing, feet, neat, quick, click*

Key Language: *What happens? What do they do on (Monday)? Do these words rhyme?*

Track: 3

How does the story help us answer our Big Question?

Listen. Point. Say.

On Thursday, we learn how to use a P. C.
It's fun and it's quick.
It takes just a click.
And there's a picture on the screen to see.

On Friday, we learn how to have fun with our friends.
We play and we share. We show that we care.
We say "See you next week!" when the school day ends.

tree

wing

Key Vocabulary: *hat, coat, bee, tree, wing, thing, feet, neat, quick, click*

Key Language: *What happens? Who are the characters? Where does the story take place?*

Track: 3

What do the children do at school?

Say. Match.

Monday	Tuesday and Wednesday	Thursday	Friday

Key Vocabulary: *learn, hang up, put, color, use, have fun, play, share, care*

Key Language: *Can you remember? What's the story about? What happens?*

Is it important to be kind?

Draw. Trace. Talk.

Be kind to others.

Key Language: *Be kind to others. How can we be kind?*

What is your favorite subject?

Listen. Say. Mark.

Science

Art

Math

Writing

Reading

Physical Education

Key Vocabulary: *Science, Art, Math, Writing, Reading, Physical Education*

Key Language: *What's your favorite subject? My favorite subject is (science).*

Track: 4

What do we have on Mondays?

Look. Say. Draw.

Monday

Tuesday

Wednesday

Thursday

Friday

Key Vocabulary: *Monday, Tuesday, Wednesday, Thursday, Friday, Science, Art, Math, Writing, Reading, Physical Education*

Key Language: *What day is today? (Monday.) What do we have on (Mondays)? We have (Art).*

What color is it?

Say. Trace. Stick.

red **orange** **yellow** **green** **blue** **purple** **pink** **black** **gray** **brown**

Key Vocabulary: *red, orange, yellow, green, blue, purple, pink, black, gray, brown*

Key Language: *What color is it? It's (red). Show me something (red). This is (red).*

What do we do at school?

Listen. Say. Trace.

use a computer

play music

speak English

paint with watercolors

read books

play in the playground

Key Vocabulary: *use a computer, play music, speak English, paint with watercolors, read books, play in the playground*

Key Language: *What do we do at school? Do we (read books)? Yes, we do. No, we don't.*

Track: 5

What does Mia do at school?

Look. Match. Say.

Key Vocabulary: *use a computer, play music, speak English, paint with watercolors, read books, play in the playground*

Key Language: *What do you do at school? I (read books). Do you (play music)? Yes, I do. No, I don't. What does (he) do at school? (He) (reads books).*

What do they need?

Listen. Circle. Say.

Key Vocabulary: *pencil, paint, book, scissors*

Key Language: *I need a pencil, please. I need some paint, please. Here you go. Thank you. What does (she) need? (She) needs a (book). She needs (scissors).*

Track: 6

How can we make the secondary colors?

Say. Paint.

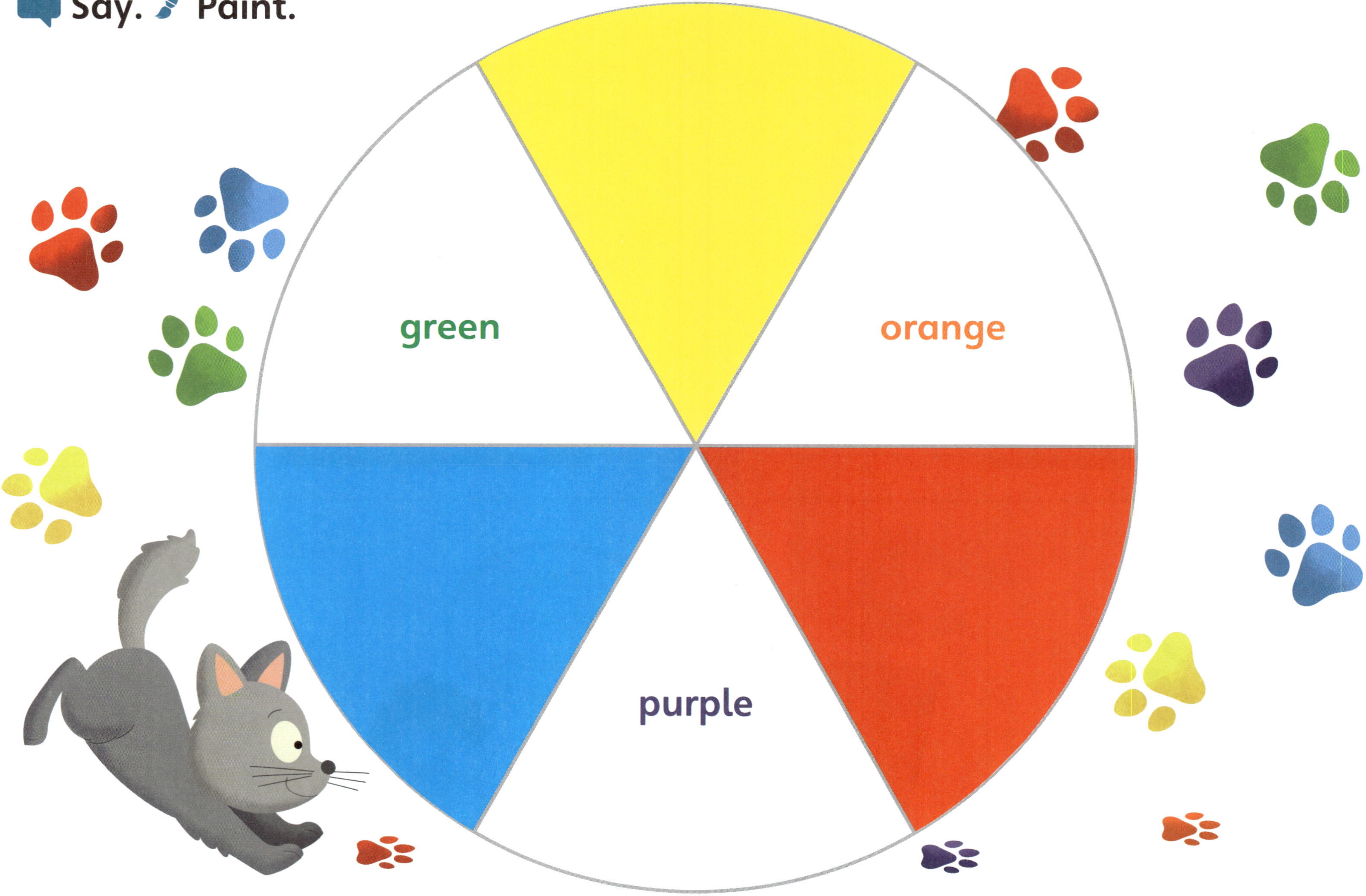

Key Vocabulary: *color wheel, primary colors, red, yellow, blue, secondary colors, orange, green, purple*

Key Language: *Mix (red) and (yellow) to make (orange).*

How many school objects can you see?

Trace. Count. Match.

5 10 15 20

Key Vocabulary: *numbers 1–20; school objects*

Key Language: *How many (erasers) can you see? Let's count: one, two, three ... nineteen, twenty.*

Look. Make. Say.

What do we do at school?

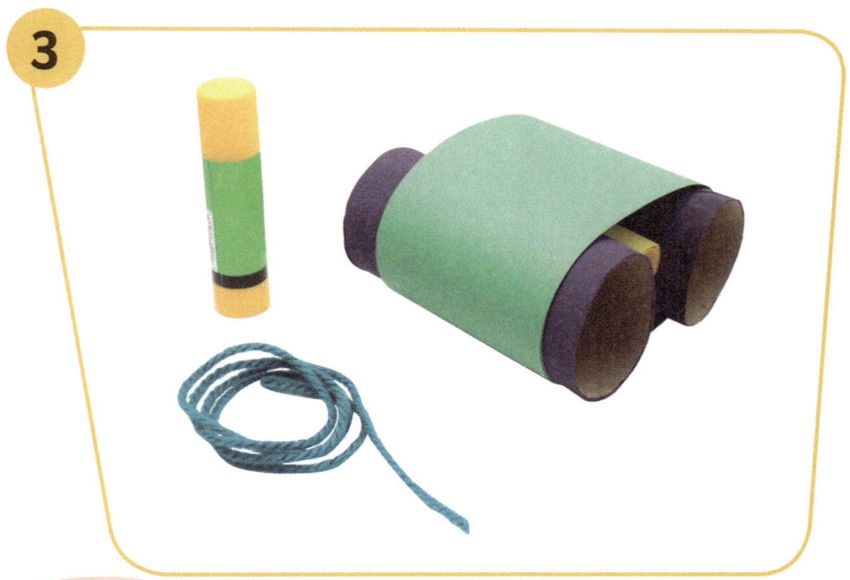

Key Vocabulary: *Monday, Tuesday, Wednesday, Thursday, Friday, Saturday, Sunday, Science, Art, Math, Writing, Reading, Physical Education, use a computer, play music, speak English, paint with watercolors, read books, play in the playground*

Key Language: *What day is it? What day is today? What's your favorite subject? My favorite subject is (Art). What do we have on Tuesdays? We have (Math) on Tuesdays. What do we do at school? We (play music). Do you (read books)? Yes, I do., No, I don't. I need a pencil, please. Here you go. Thank you.*

2 How can we show our feelings?

Listen. Say. Sing.

scared

excited

surprised

bored

shy

silly

Key Vocabulary: *scared, excited, surprised, bored, shy, silly*

Tracks: 7 and 8

What is the story about?

Listen. Say. Point.

Maddy Goes to a Party

cake

Key Vocabulary: *birthday, party, worried, sad, scary, fun, fix, bake, cake, wait*

Key Language: *Who are the characters? How do the characters feel? Do these words rhyme?*

Track: 9

How does the story help us answer our Big Question?

Listen. Point. Say.

Key Vocabulary: *birthday, party, worried, sad, scary, fun, fix, cake, bake, wait*

Key Language: *What happens (first)?*

Track: 9

Can you remember how the characters feel?

Point. Say. Draw.

1

2

3

4

Key Vocabulary: *birthday, party, worried, sad, scary, fun, fix, cake, bake, wait*

Key Language: *Can you remember? Think about what happens first. How does s/he feel?*

Is it important to talk about our feelings?

Draw. Trace. Talk.

Talk about your feelings.

Key Vocabulary: *sad, bored, scared, shy*

Key Language: *How does (he) feel? (He) feels (sad). How do you feel? I feel (scared).*

How do we show our feelings?

Listen. Say. Trace.

1

scream

2

jump up and down

3

shout hooray

4

yawn

5

cry

6

laugh

Key Vocabulary: *scream, jump up and down, shout hooray, yawn, cry, laugh*
Key Language: *How do we show our feelings?*
Track: 10

How can you show your feelings?

Look. Follow. Say.

Key Vocabulary: *happy, bored, surprised, sad, scared, excited, feelings, scream, jump up and down, shout hooray, yawn, cry, laugh*

Key Language: *How does (Mia) feel? (She)'s (happy). What do you do when you're (bored)? When I'm (bored), I (yawn).*

What feeling comes next?

Look. Say. Stick.

1

2

3

Key Vocabulary: *feelings, happy, bored, surprised, sad, scared, excited, pattern*

Key Language: *What comes next?*

What can we see at a birthday party?

Color. Trace. Listen.

candy

cake

candle

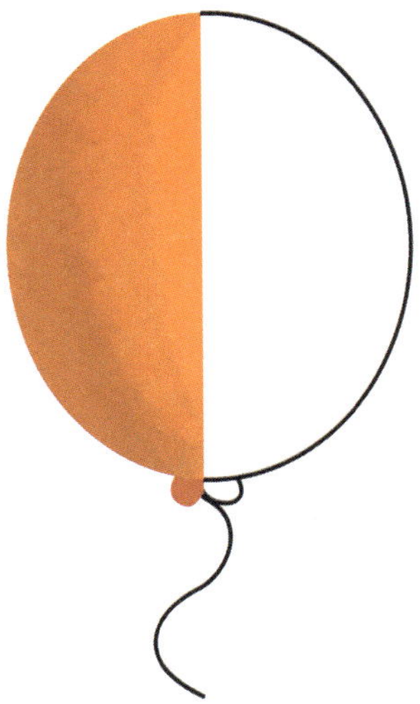

balloon

present

party hat

Key Vocabulary: *candy, cake, candle, balloon, present, party hat, feelings*

Key Language: *Do you like birthday parties? How do you feel? How do you show how your feelings?*

Track: 11

Can you find the differences?

Look. Say. Circle.

Key Vocabulary: *present, balloon, cake, party hat, candy, party*

Key Language: *Can you find the differences? What's different? How many ...? What color ...?*

How old are you?

Listen. Say. Draw.

1

2

3

4

Key Language: *How old are you? I'm (five) years old.*

Track: 12

Can you decorate the birthday cakes?

Look. Color. Trace.

1

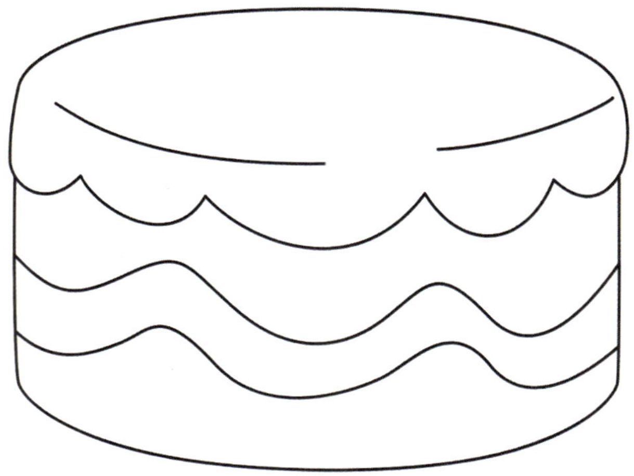

brown

2

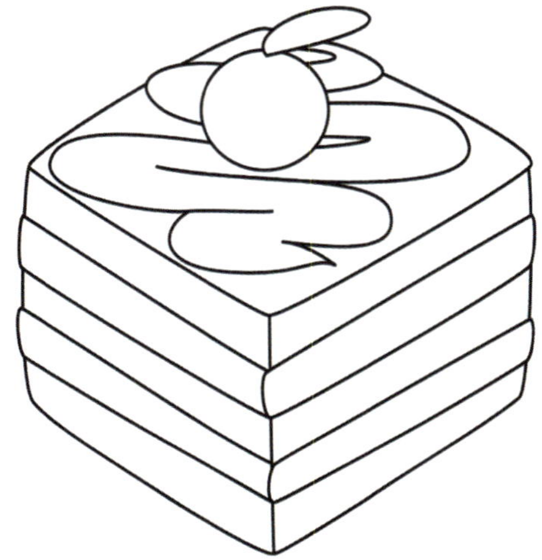

pink

3

white

4

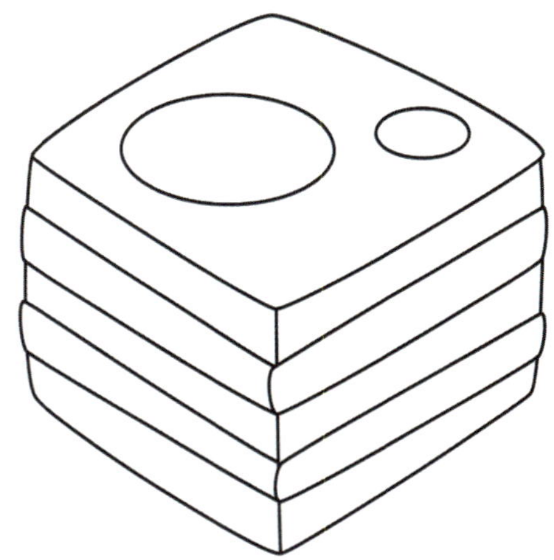

gray

Key Vocabulary: *brown, pink, white, gray, decorate*

Key Language: *Color (the cakes). Decorate (the cakes).*

How many candles can you see?

Trace. Count. Draw.

30

Key Vocabulary: *numbers 1–20, thirty*

Key Language: *How many (candles) can you see? Let's count: one, two, three ..., twenty ..., thirty. Sets of ten. Three sets of ten.*

Look. Make. Say.

How can we show our feelings?

1

2

3

4

Key Vocabulary: *scared, excited, surprised, bored, shy, silly, scream, jump up and down, shout hooray, yawn, cry, laugh, candy, cake, candle, balloon, present, party hat, birthday party*

Key Language: *When we're (bored), we yawn. What do you do when you're (scared)? When I'm (scared), I (scream). How old are you? I'm (five) years old.*

3 How are we the same or different?

Listen. Say. Sing.

child

children

woman

women

man

men

Key Vocabulary: *child, children, woman, women, man, men*

Tracks: 13 and 14

What is the story about?

Listen. Say. Point.

The Kindergarten Photograph

line up

tie

Key Vocabulary: *line up, tie, glasses, eye doctor, dress, new, different, cry, hug, great*

Key Language: *Who are the characters? How does Joana feel? Why do you think she's crying?*

Track: 15

How does the story help us answer our Big Question?

Listen. Say. Point.

Key Vocabulary: *line up, tie, glasses, eye doctor, dress, new, different, cry, hug, great*

Key Language: *What's Joana wearing? Where is she? Who has (long) hair?*

Track: 15

Can you remember the story? What's wrong with the scenes?

Look. Say. Circle.

1

2

3

4

Key Vocabulary: *line up, tie, glasses, eye doctor, dress, new, different, cry, hug, great*

Key Language: *Can you remember the story? What's different? Is this the same? What's wrong with this scene?*

Is it important to be proud of ourselves?

Draw. Trace. Talk.

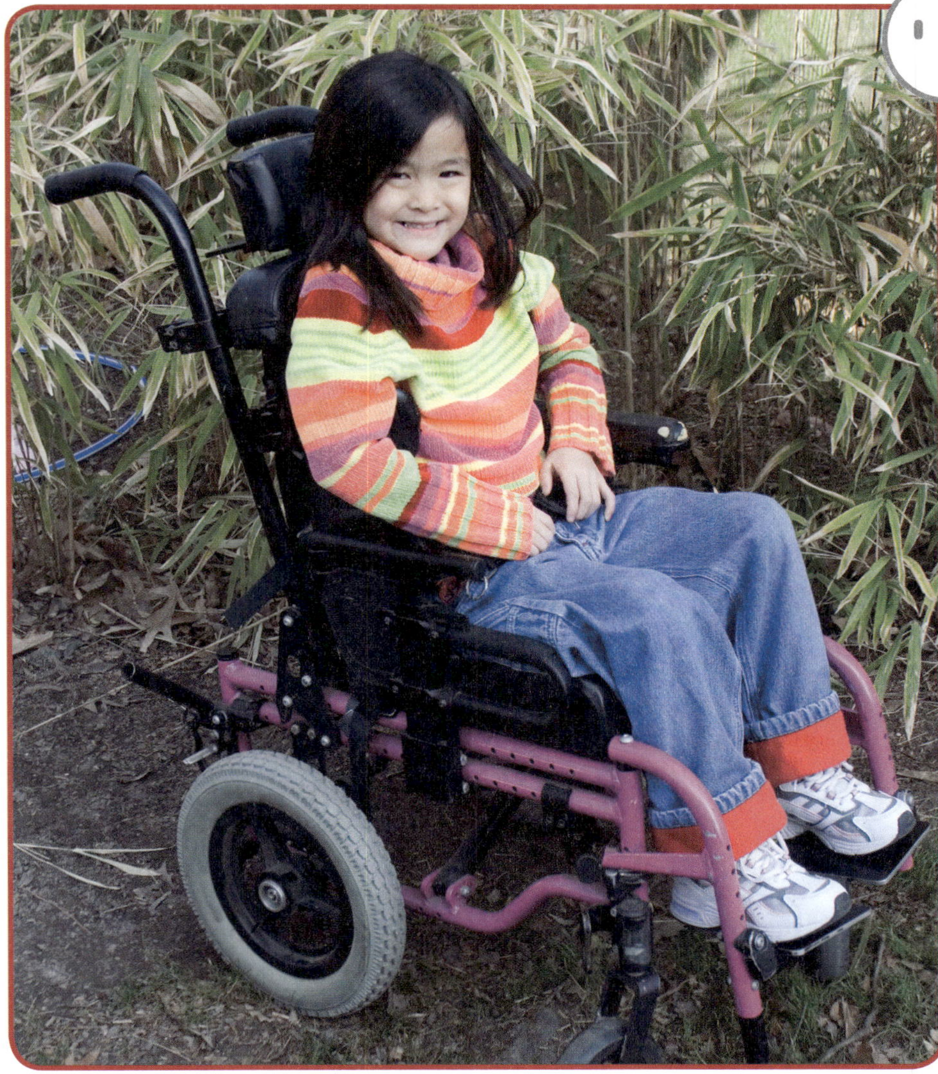

Be proud of yourself.

Key Language: *Be proud of yourself. I'm proud of myself.*

How is Leo's family the same and different?

Say. Listen. Trace.

tall short thin aunt cousin uncle

Key Vocabulary: *tall, short, thin, uncle, aunt, cousin*
Key Language: *Who's this? Who's (tall)?*
Track: 16

What does Mia's family look like?

Look. Say. Mark.

Key Vocabulary: *tall, short, thin, woman, girl, man, boy, men, women, children*

Key Language: *What does (she) look like? S/he's (tall). She's a (woman). He's a (boy). How many (men) can you see?*

Who is the tallest?

Point. Say.

1 Their cousin is ...

2 Leo is ...

3 Mia is ...

Key Vocabulary: *short, shorter, the shortest, tall, taller, the tallest*

Key Language: *Who is the (shortest)? (Mia) is the (shortest).*

What does your hair look like?

Listen. Color. Trace.

1

blond

2

red

3

long

4

short

5

curly

6

straight

Key Vocabulary: *blond, red, long, short, curly, straight*

Key Language: *What does your hair look like? It's (long). What color is (her) hair? What color is your hair? It's (red).*

Track: 17

What does he look like?

Point. Write. Say.

Key Vocabulary: *short, tall, thin, long, curly, straight, blond, red, brown, black, hair*

Key Language: *What does (she) look like? (She)'s (short). (She) has (curly) (black) hair. Who is it?*

What's your name?

Listen. Circle. Say.

1 What's your name?

Leo. Ben.

2 What's your mother's name?

Amy. Kim.

3 What's your father's name?

Dan. Tom.

4 What's your favorite color?

Key Language: *What's your name? My name is... What's your (mother)'s name? My (mother)'s name is ... What's your favorite color? My favorite color is...*

Track: 18

What does your family tree look like?

Draw. Write. Say. Stick.

Key Vocabulary: *family tree, sister, brother, mother, father, aunt, uncle, cousin, grandmother, grandfather*

Key Language: *Who's this? This is my (sister). (Her) name is ...*

How many children can you see?

Trace. Count. Draw.

40

Look. Make. Say.

How are we the same or different?

1

2

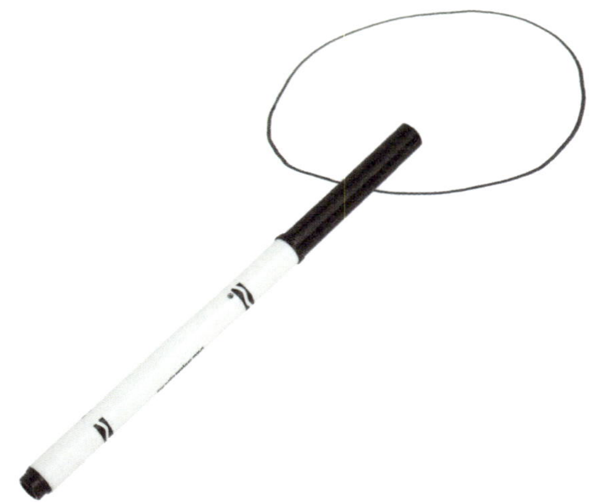

Key Vocabulary: *child, children, woman, women, man, men, aunt, uncle, cousin, grandmother, grandfather, tall, short, thin, blond, red, long, short, curly, straight*

Key Language: *What do you look like? What color is your hair? I have (black curly hair). What does s/he look like? She's a (woman). She's (tall and thin). She has (short) (red) hair. What's (her) name? (Her) name is ...*

3

4

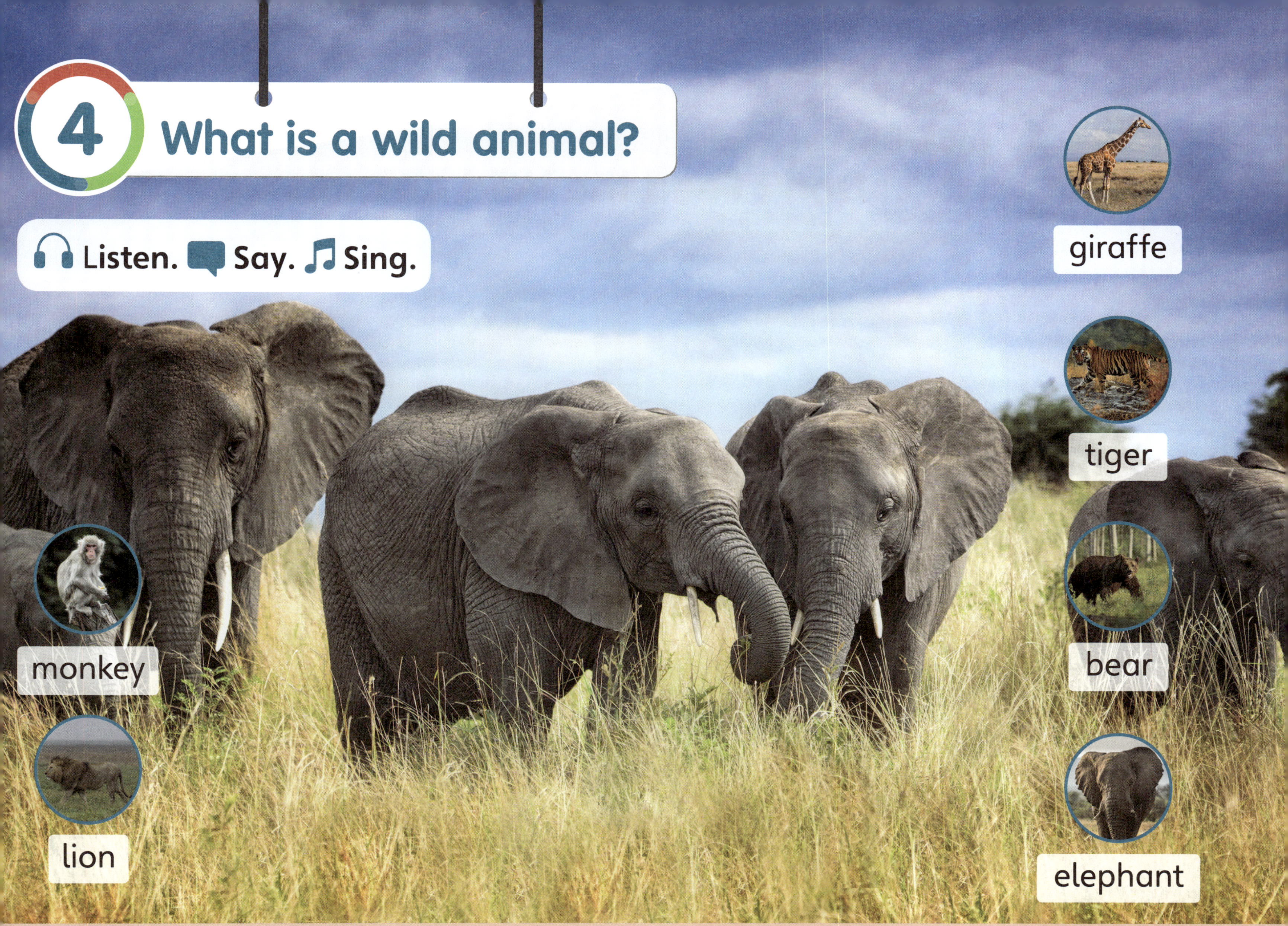

4 What is a wild animal?

Listen. Say. Sing.

monkey

lion

giraffe

tiger

bear

elephant

Key Vocabulary: *monkey, lion, giraffe, tiger, bear, elephant*

Tracks: 19 and 20

What is the story about?

Listen. Look. Say.

Don't Feed the Wild Animals

cute

rule

Sue

Key Vocabulary: *cute, rule, Sue, feed, wild animals, rhino, horns, stripes, cub, claws, teeth*

Key Language: *What do you think the story is about? Is it about pets? It's about (wild animals).*

Track: 21

How does the story help us answer our Big Question?

Listen. Point. Say.

Key Vocabulary: *cute, rule, Sue, feed, wild animals, rhino, horns, stripes, cub, claws, teeth*

Key Language: *Where are they? What's the name of the safari? What are the rules? How many elephants are there?*

Track: 21

What happens first, next, and last?

Look. Say. Write.

Key Vocabulary: *cute, rule, Sue, feed, wild animals, rhino, horns, stripes, cub, claws, teeth*

Key Language: *What happens first? What happens next? What happens at the end?*

Is it important to protect wild animals?

Draw. Talk. Trace.

Pick up garbage.

Key Language: *Protect wild animals. Pick up garbage.*

Can you name the animals?

Listen. Circle. Trace.

1 snake

2 whale

3 eagle

4 shark

5 kangaroo

6 toucan

Key Vocabulary: *snake, whale, eagle, shark, kangaroo, toucan*

Track: 22

Where does this animal belong?

Look. Say. Stick.

Key Vocabulary: *snake, toucan, shark, eagle, whale, kangaroo, air, land, water*

Key Language: *Where does this animal go? On land. In the air. In the water.*

How many tigers are there?

Count. Circle. Say.

 +  = 5 | 6 | 7

 +  = 4 | 5 | 6

 +  = 6 | 7 | 8

 +  = 7 | 8 | 9

Key Vocabulary: *tiger, whale, giraffe, toucan*

Key Language: *How many (tigers) are there in this group? Let's count. (Two) plus (four) equals (six). There are (six) (tigers).*

What part is each animal missing?

Match. Listen. Trace.

paw fin beak trunk tail wing

Key Vocabulary: *paw, fin, beak, trunk, tail, wing*
Key Language: *What's missing?*
Track: 23

What does an elephant look like?

Look. Say. Circle.

Key Vocabulary: *big, small, long, trunk, neck, tail, fin, beak, ears, paws, wings, colors*

Key Language: *What does a (whale) look like? It's (big). It's (gray.) It has a (small) (fin). It has (big) (ears).*

Do you like these wild animals?

Say. Listen. Color.

1

Do you like bears?

2

Do you like toucans?

3

Do you like monkeys?

4

Do you like snakes?

Key Vocabulary: *bear, toucan, monkey, snake, cute, funny, scary, colorful*

Key Language: *Do you like (bears)? Yes, I do. No, I don't. Why? Why not? Because they are (cute).*

Track: 24

Can you describe a bear?

Look. Circle. Say.

1 This is a ...

bear.

whale.

2 It is ...

blue.

brown.

2 It eats ...

fish.

bananas.

2 It lives in the ...

forest.

ocean.

Key Vocabulary: *bear, whale, fish, banana, forest, ocean, colors*

Key Language: *This is a (bear). It's (brown). It eats (fish). It lives in the (forest).*

How many fish can you see?

Trace. Count. Draw.

50

Look. Make. Say.

What is a wild animal?

1

2

3

4

Key Vocabulary: *wild animals, monkey, lion, giraffe, tiger, bear, elephant, snake, whale, eagle, shark, kangaroo, toucan, on land, in the air, in the water, paw, fin, neck, beak, trunk, tail, wing, big, small, long, short, forest, ocean*

Key Language: *Where does (a shark) belong? (In the water.) What does a (giraffe) look like? (It's big). It's (brown). It has a (long neck). This is a (bear). It's (brown). It eats (fish). It lives in the (forest).*

5 Who works in our community?

Listen. Say. Sing.

firefighter

doctor

chef

police officer

mail carrier

cashier

Key Vocabulary: *firefighter, doctor, chef, police officer, mail carrier, cashier*

Tracks: 25 and 26

What is the story about?

Listen. Point.

hose

Jewel Goes to School

Key Vocabulary: *bow, froze, hose, snow, furry, cool, strong, still, quiet, proud*

Key Language: *What do you think the story is about? Who is Jewel? Is there a (girl) in the story?*

Track: 27

How does the story help us answer our Big Question?

Listen. Point. Say.

Key Vocabulary: *bow, froze, hose, snow, furry, cool, strong, still, quiet, proud*

Key Language: *Who are the characters? Who is furry? Who is proud? Why is she proud?*

Track: 27

Who does it belong to?

Look. Say. Match.

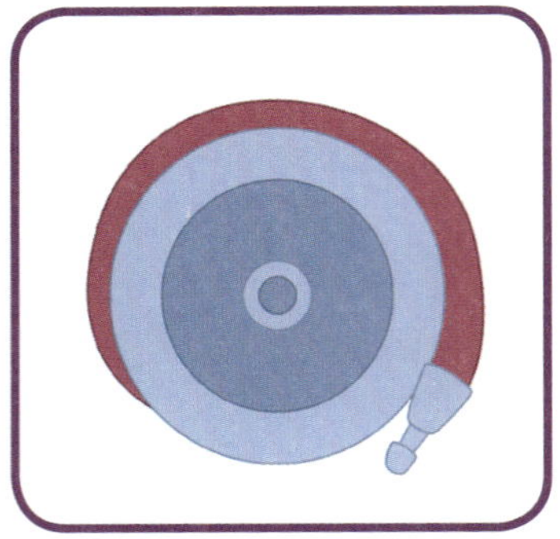

Key Vocabulary: *bow, froze, hose, snow, furry, cool, strong, still, quiet, proud*

Key Language: *Can you remember? Who does it belong to? It belongs to (the girl).*

Is it important to respect people working in our community?

Draw. **Trace.** **Talk.**

Respect people in your community.

Key Vocabulary: *respect, community, polite, listen, say*

Key Language: *Be polite. Say "thank you." Listen. Show respect.*

Where do people work?

Listen. Follow. Trace.

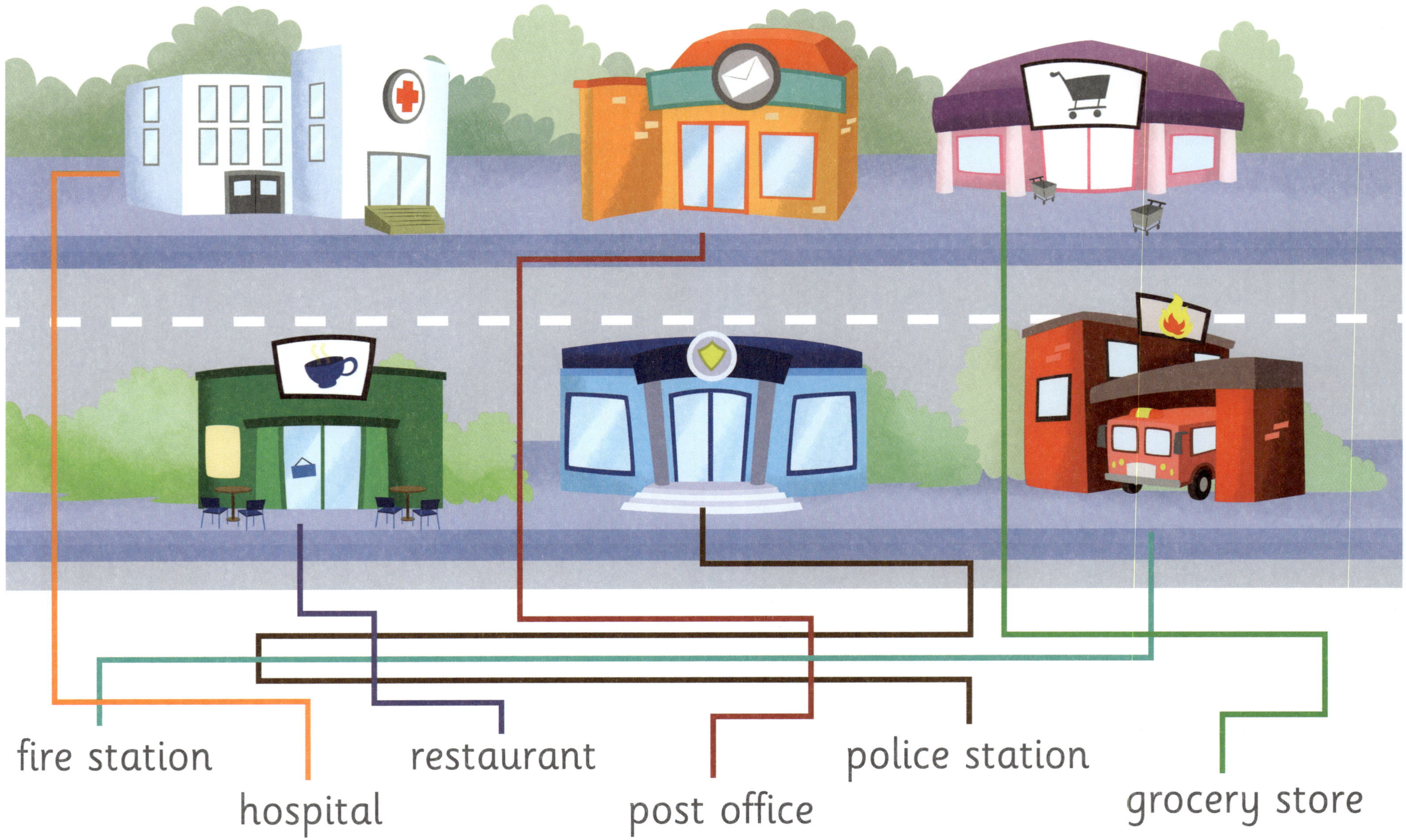

Key Vocabulary: *fire station, hospital, restaurant, post office, police station, grocery store, town, city*

Key Language: *Where do people work?*

Track: 28

Where do they work?

Look. Say. Stick.

Key Vocabulary: *fire station, hospital, restaurant, post office, police station, grocery store, firefighter, doctor, chef, police officer, mail carrier, cashier*

Key Language: *Where does a (firefighter) work? S/he works in a (fire station). A firefighter works in a fire station.*

How many more?

Count. Draw. Trace.

 + ☐ = 10

 + ☐ = 8

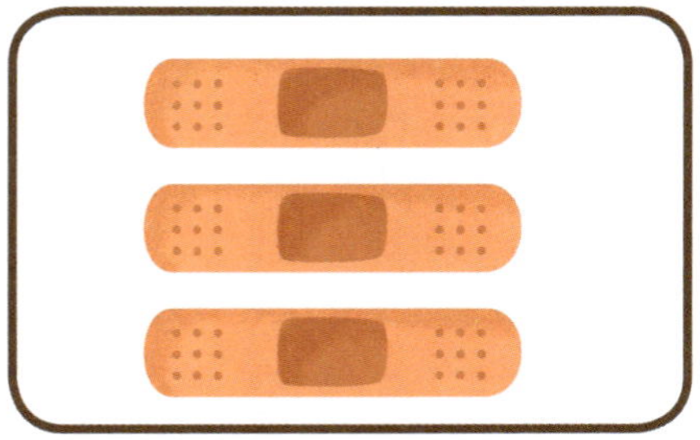 + ☐ = 7

 + ☐ = 5

Key Vocabulary: *numbers 1–10*

Key Language: *How many more? (Five) plus (five) equals (ten).*

What do they do?

Listen. Color. Trace.

put out fires

take care of people

cook food

keep people safe

deliver mail

ring up groceries

Key Vocabulary: *put out fires, take care of people, cook food, keep people safe, deliver mail, ring up groceries*

Key Language: *What do (firefighters) do? They (put out fires).*

Track: 29

Who's she?

Look. Say. Color.

Key Vocabulary: *put out fires, take care of people, cook food, keep people safe, deliver mail, ring up groceries, jobs*

Key Language: *Who's he? He's a (doctor). Where does he work? (He) works in (a hospital) What does he do? (He) (takes care of people).*

What do you want to be?

Listen. Match. Talk.

Key Vocabulary: *jobs, why, because*

Key Language: *What do you want to be? I want to be a ... Why? Because I love to ...*

Track: 30

What do you want to be?

Paint. Say.

Key Language: *What do you want to be? I want to be a (doctor).*

How many people can you see?

Trace. Count. Draw.

60

Look. Make. Say.

Who works in our community?

1

2

3

4

Key Vocabulary: *firefighter, doctor, chef, police officer, mail carrier, cashier, fire station, hospital, restaurant, police station, post office, grocery store, put out fires, take care of people, keep people safe, deliver mail, ring up groceries*

Key Language: *Where does s/he work? S/he works in a ... A (chef) works in a (restaurant). What do (chefs) do? They (cook food).*

6 Why are restaurants special?

Listen. Say. Sing.

Key Vocabulary: *waiter, menu, drink, main dish, side dish, dessert*

Tracks: 31 and 32

What is the story about?

Listen. Point. Say.

Uncle Piero's Special Restaurant

meet

teach

Key Vocabulary: *meet, teach, see, eat, cook, was, knead, salad, bread, restaurant*

Key Language: *Where do they go? Who is Piero? What does he teach them?*

Track: 33

How does the story help us answer our Big Question?

Listen. Point. Say.

see

eat

Key Vocabulary: *meet, teach, see, eat, cook, was, knead, salad, bread, restaurant*

Key Language: *Who are the characters? What happens? Where does the story take place?*

Track: 33

Can you answer the questions?

Say. Point. Match.

1 Where does the story take place?

2 Who are the characters?

3 What happens at the restaurant?

Key Vocabulary: *meet, teach, see, eat, cook, was, knead, salad, bread, restaurant*

Key Language: *Who are the characters? What happens? Where does the story take place?*

Is it important to be polite in restaurants?

Draw. Trace. Talk.

Be polite in restaurants.

Key Language: *Be polite. Is it polite? Yes, it is. No, it isn't.*

Can you name the food?

Listen. Match. Trace.

Key Vocabulary: *steak, beans, lemonade, rice, soda, French fries*

Key Language: *Do you like (beans)? What's your favorite?*

Track: 34

Do you like beans?

✓ **Mark.** ✗ **Cross.** **Say.**

Food	Me	My Friend

Key Vocabulary: *beans, soda, rice, French fries, steak*

Key Language: *Do you like (beans)? Yes, I do. No, I don't. I like (soda). I don't like (beans). (Sara) likes (beans). (She) doesn't like (soda).*

Which plate has more?

Count. Point. Draw.

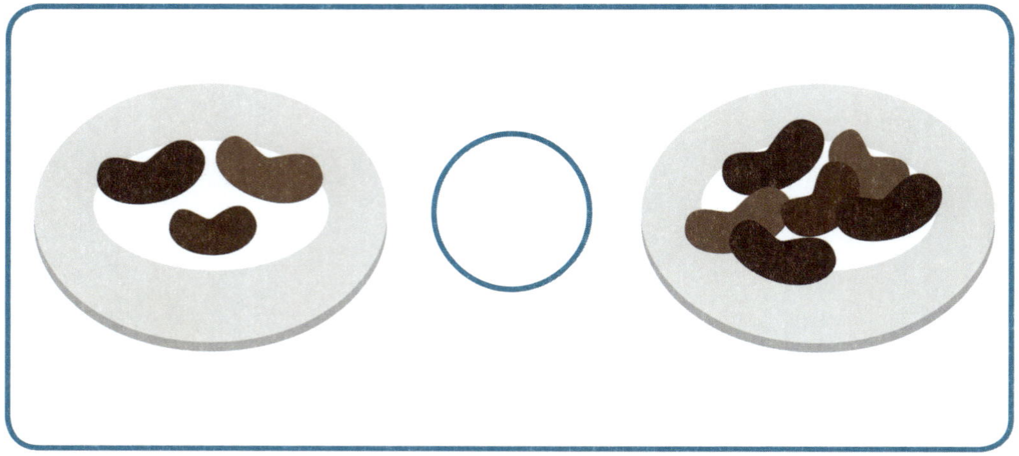

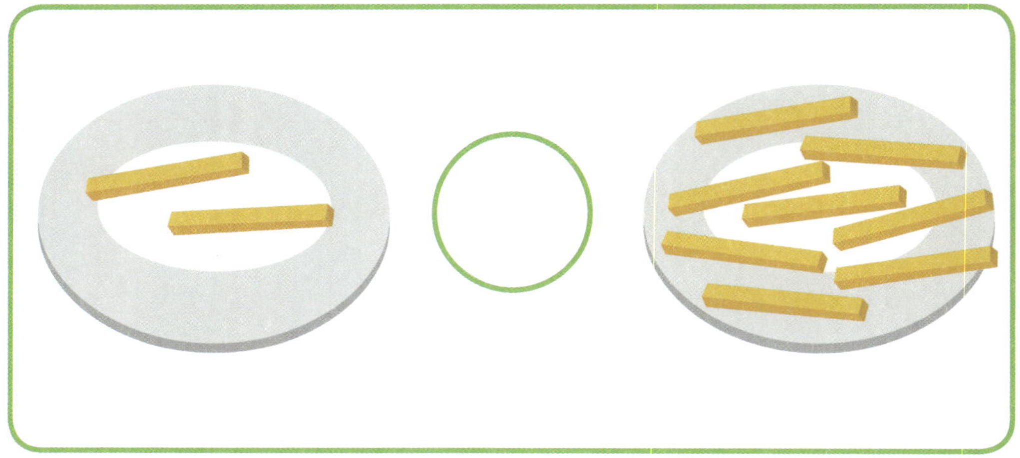

Key Vocabulary: *more, less*

Key Language: *How many? Let's count. Which has more? (Six) is more than (three).*

Can you name the food?

Listen. Stick. Trace.

spaghetti

pizza

ice cream

chocolate cake

vegetables

cheeseburger

Key Vocabulary: *spaghetti, pizza, ice cream, chocolate cake, vegetables, cheeseburger*

Track: 35

What do we need to eat spaghetti?

Say. Read. Draw.

1 We need a  and a 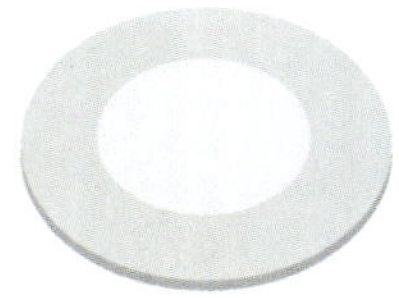 to eat .

2 We need a  and a  to eat .

3 We need a 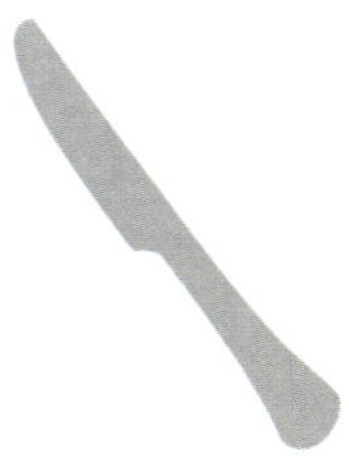 and a  to eat .

4 We need a ☐ and ☐ to eat ☐.

Key Vocabulary: *fork, knife, spoon, plate, bowl, spaghetti, soup, steak*

Key Language: *What do we need to eat (steak)? We need a (knife) and a (fork) to eat (steak).*

What would you like?

Say. Listen. Color.

Drinks

Main Dishes

Side Dishes

Desserts

Key Vocabulary: *water, orange juice, soda, lemonade, fish, pizza, spaghetti, vegetables, French fries, soup, salad, ice cream, cookies, cake*

Key Language: *What would you like? I would like (pizza), please. Anything else? No, thank you.*

Track: 36

Is it a fruit or a vegetable?

Say. Color.

green = vegetable
red = fruit

Key Vocabulary: *banana, lettuce, grapes, orange, onion, pear, carrot, pineapple, apple, broccoli, fruit, vegetable*

Key Language: *Is it a fruit or a vegetable? I think it's a (fruit).*

How many drinks can you see?

Trace. Count. Draw.

70

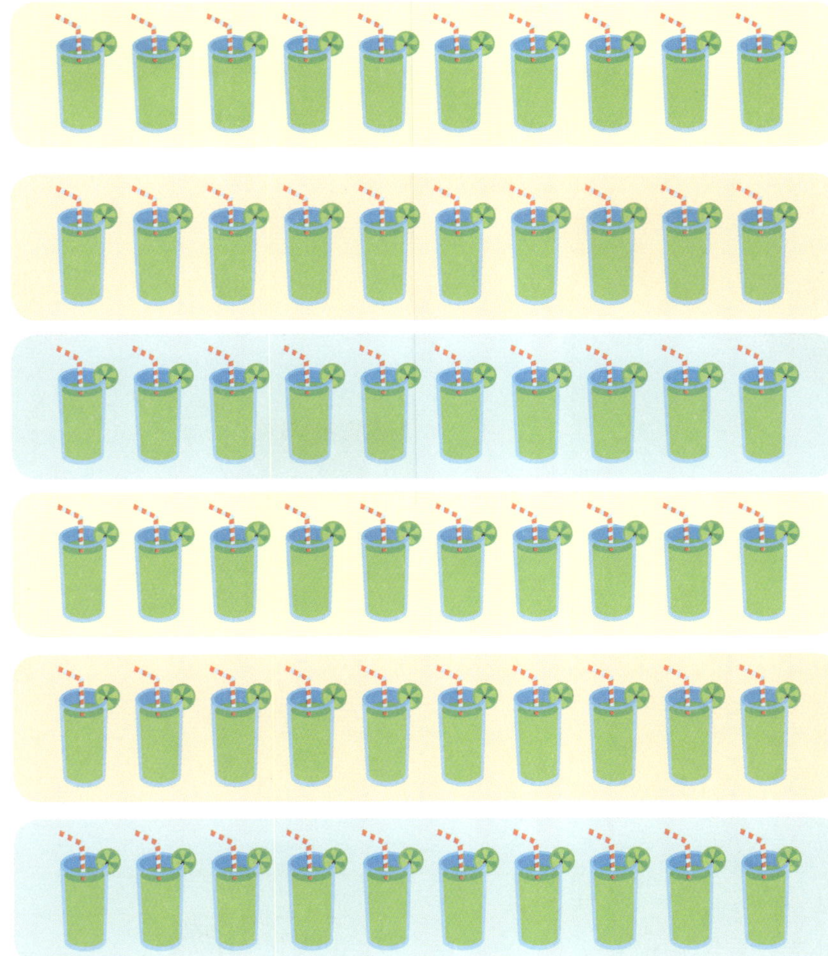

Key Vocabulary: *ten, twenty, thirty, forty, fifty, sixty, seventy*

Key Language: *How many (drinks) can you see? Let's count by tens. Sets of ten. Seven sets of ten.*

Look. Make. Say.

Why are restaurants special?

1

2

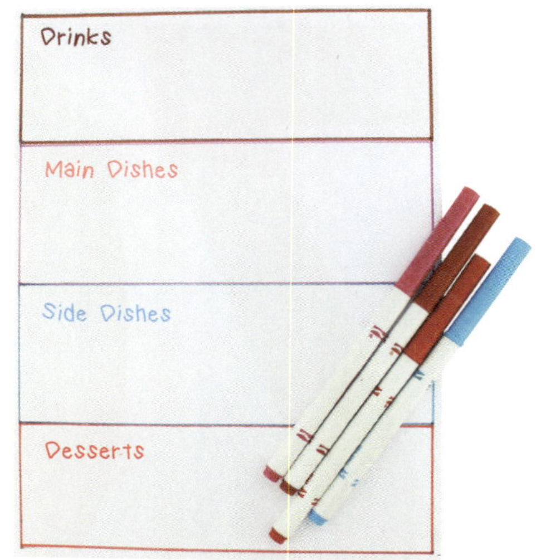

3

4

Key Vocabulary: *waiter, menu, drink, main dish, side dish, dessert, steak, beans, rice, French fries, soda, lemonade, spaghetti, pizza, ice cream, chocolate cake, vegetables, cheeseburger, spoon, fork, knife, bowl plate.*

Key Language: *Do you like (beans)? Yes, I do. No, I don't. I like (beans), I don't like (soda), She likes (steak). She doesn't like (rice). We need a (fork) and a (plate) to eat (spaghetti). What would you like for (a side dish)? Would you like (steak) for (a main dish)? Yes, please. No, thank you. (She) has (ice cream) for (dessert).*

7 What does a routine look like?

Listen. Say. Sing.

get up

get dressed

have breakfast

go to school

go home

do homework

Key Vocabulary: *get up, get dressed, have breakfast, go to school, go home, do homework*

Tracks: 37 and 38

What is the story about?

Listen. Point. Say.

The Hare and the Tortoise

clock

clothes

cry

Key Vocabulary: *clock, clothes, cry, tree, nap, fast, slow, far, shell, race*

Key Language: *Why doesn't Tortoise have to get dressed? (Because he has a shell.) Why does Hare think he will win? (Because he can run very fast.)*

Track: 39

How does the story help us answer our Big Question?

Listen. Point. Say.

Key Vocabulary: *clock, clothes, cry, tree, nap, fast, slow, far, shell, race*

Key Language: *What happens (first)? What happens at the end? Who says, "Don't cry, my friend"?*

Track: 39

Can you put the story in order?

Look. Write. Say.

Key Vocabulary: *clock, clothes, cry, tree, nap, fast, slow, far, shell, race*

Key Language: *Put the story in order. What happens (first)? What happens at the end?*

Is it important to follow a routine?

Draw. Trace. Talk.

Follow a routine.

Key Vocabulary: *routine, morning, afternoon, evening*

Key Language: *Follow a routine. What do you do in the (morning)?Is (she) following a healthy routine?*

What do they do after school?

Listen. Say. Trace.

dance class

soccer practice

music lessons

swimming lessons

play with friends

gymnastics

Key Vocabulary: *dance class, soccer practice, music lessons, swimming lessons, play with friends, gymnastics*

Key Language: *What do you do after school? I (go to dance class). What does (he) do? (He) (plays with friends).*

Track: 40

What do you do after school?

Draw. Stick. Say.

Key Vocabulary: *What do you do after school? I (have swimming lessons). What does (she) do after school? (She) (has soccer practice).*

What happens when you take away one?

Count. Say. Write.

4 – 1

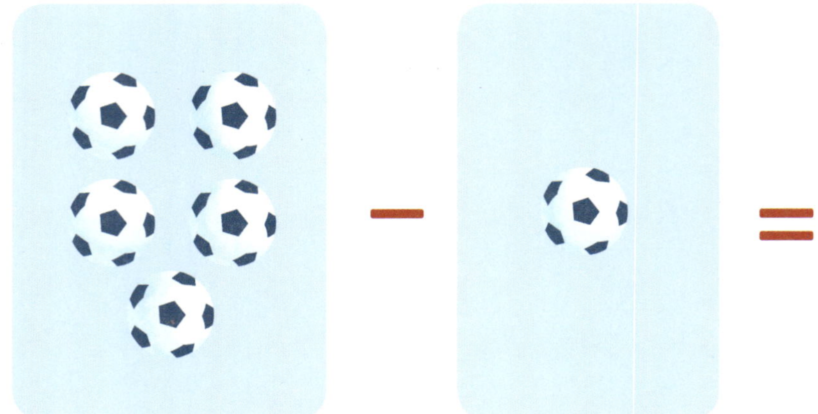

5 – 1

3 – 1

2 – 1

Key Vocabulary: *take away one, minus, numbers*

Key Language: *(Four) minus (one) equals (three).*

What do you do in the evening?

Listen. Circle. Trace.

Yes No

eat dinner

Yes No

take a bath

Yes No

brush teeth

Yes No

put on pajamas

Yes No

read a book

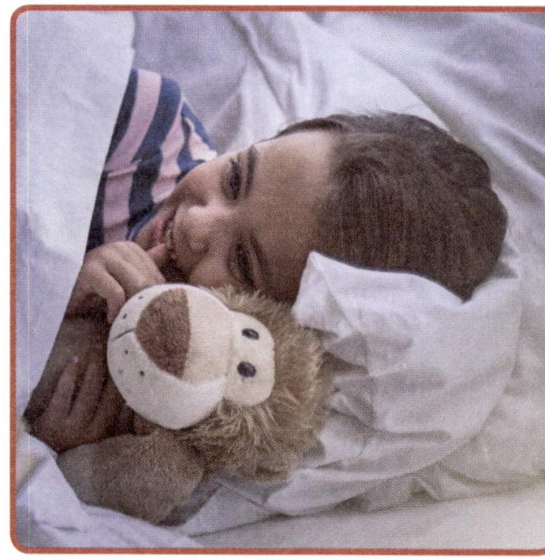

Yes No

go to bed

Key Vocabulary: *eat dinner, take a bath, brush teeth, put on pajamas, read a book, go to bed*

Key Language: *Do you eat dinner in the evening? Yes, I do. No, I don't.*

Track: 41

Do you always brush your teeth?

Draw. Color. Say.

✓✓ ✓ ✗

✓✓ ✓ ✗

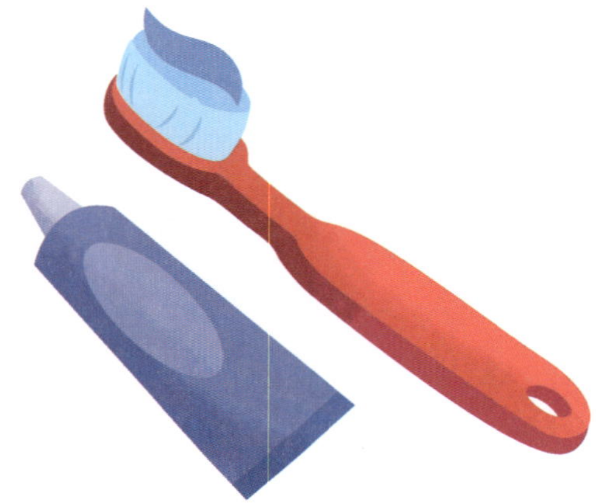

✓✓ ✓ ✗

✓✓ ✓ ✗

✓✓ ✓ ✗

Key Vocabulary: *eat dinner, brush teeth, put on pajamas, go to bed, always, sometimes, never*

Key Language: *What do you do in the evening? I always brush my teeth. I sometimes read a book. I never take a bath in the evening.*

What do you want to do?

Listen. Circle. Say.

Key Vocabulary: *bored, listen to music, play soccer, play a game. eat ice cream, read a book, paint*

Key Language: *I'm bored. What do you want to do? I don't know. Let's (paint).*

Track: 42

What time is it?

Say. Draw.

1

2

3

4

5

Key Vocabulary: *o'clock, minute hand, hour hand*

Key Language: *What time is it? It's (ten) o'clock.*

How many can you see?

Trace. Count. Draw.

80

Key Vocabulary: *ten, twenty, thirty, forty, fifty, sixty, seventy, eighty*

Key Language: *How many (toothbrushes) can you see? Let's count by tens. Sets of ten. Eight sets of ten.*

Look. Make. Say.

What does a routine look like?

1

2

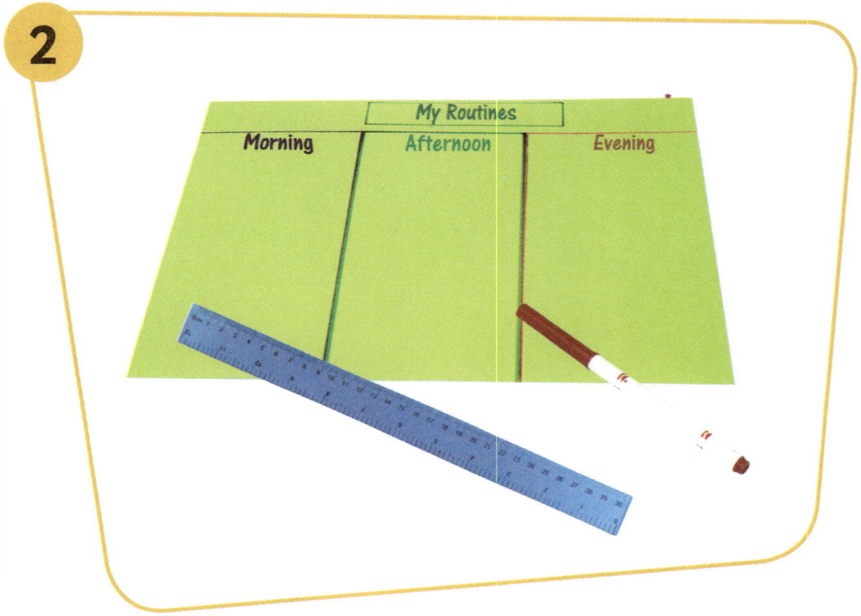

Key Vocabulary: *get up, get dressed, have breakfast, go to school, go home, do homework, dance class, soccer practice, music lessons, swimming lessons, gymnastics, play with friends, have dinner, take a bath, brush teeth, put on pajamas, read a book, go to bed, evening, always, sometimes, never*

Key Language: *What do you do after school? I have (dance class). I (play with friends). What do you do in the evening? I (have dinner). I (sometimes) (read a book).*

3

4

8 How can we care for the Earth?

Listen. Say. Sing.

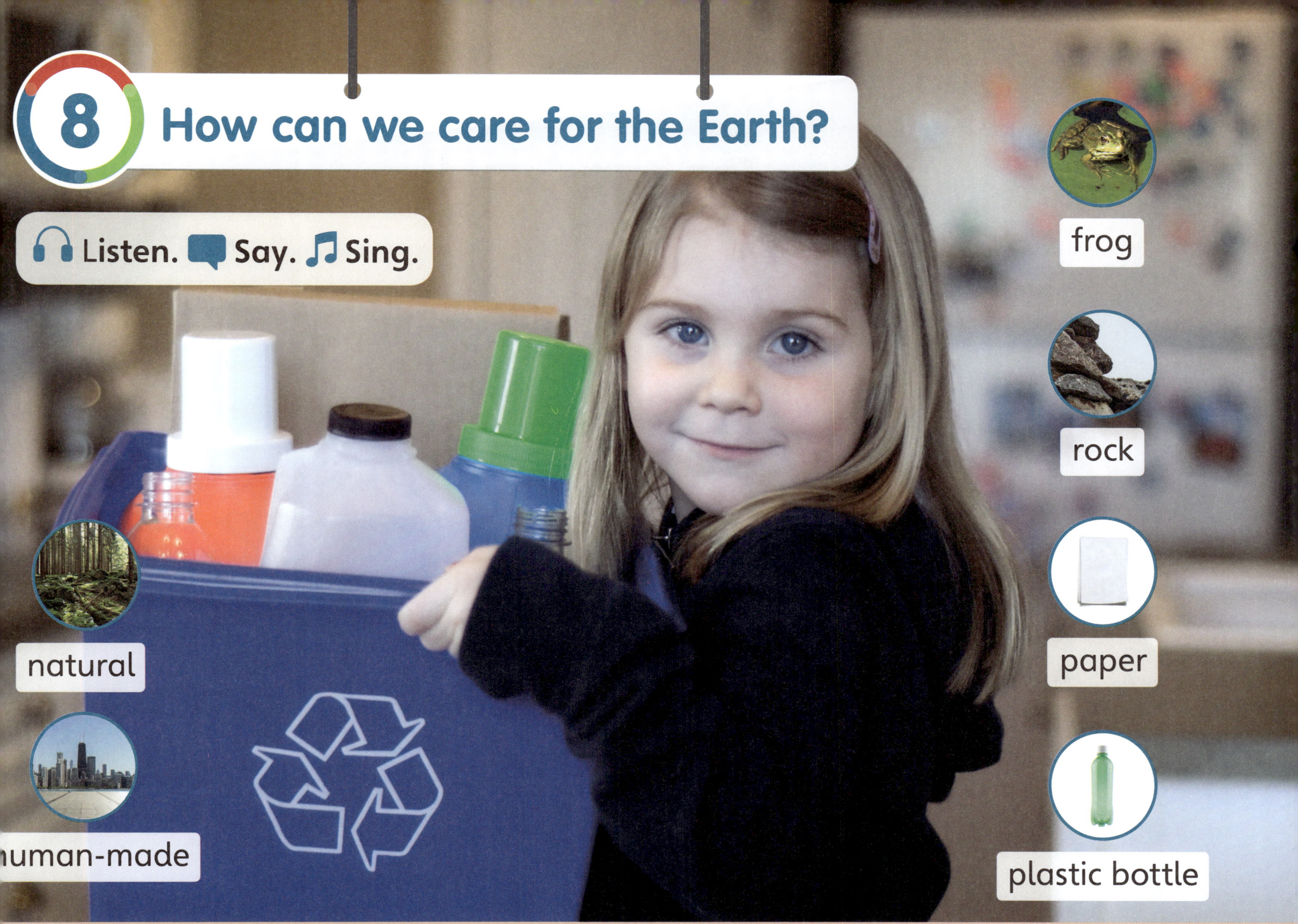

Key Vocabulary: *natural, human-made, frog, rock, paper, plastic bottle*

Tracks: 43 and 44

What is the story about?

Listen. Point. Say.

The Yard Guard

Stevie

fly

Key Vocabulary: *Stevie, fly, smart, squirrel, stand, scatter, worm, seed, ground, peanut, guard*

Key Language: *Where is (Stevie)? What does he learn at school? Who is surprised? Why is Stevie the yard guard?*

Track: 45

How does the story help us answer our Big Question?

Listen. Point. Say.

Stevie gets some seeds and scatters them on the ground.

Stevie sees two squirrels.
He gets some peanuts for the squirrels.

squirrel

stand

scatter

Key Vocabulary: *Stevie, fly, smart, squirrel, stand, scatter, worm, seed, ground, peanut, guard*

Key Language: *Who are the characters? What happens? Where does the story take place?*

Track: 45

What happens in the story?

Look. Read. Match.

1  waters the 

2  sees two 

3  feeds the 

4  is the guardian of the 

Key Vocabulary: *Stevie, fly, smart, squirrel, stand, scatter, worm, seed, ground, peanut, guard*

Key Language: *What happens? Let's tell the story.*

Is it important to save water?

Draw. Trace. Talk.

Don't waste water.

Key Vocabulary: *water, faucet, waste, save, watering can*

Key Language: *Save water. Don't waste water.*

Can you name the human-made objects?

Listen. Color. Trace.

Key

1 = red

2 = gray

3 = brown

4 = blue

5 = green

6 = yellow

1
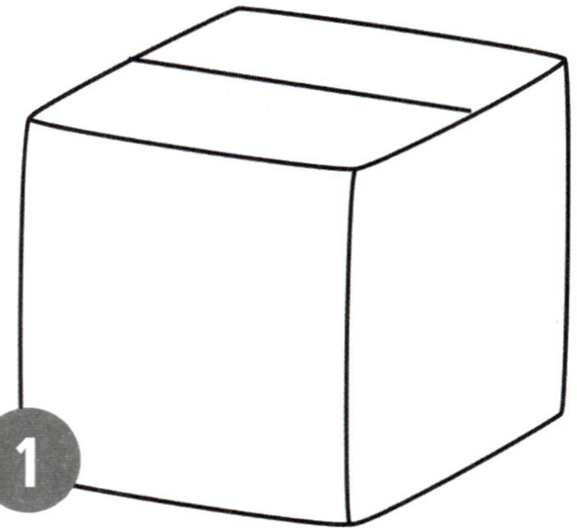
cardboard box

2
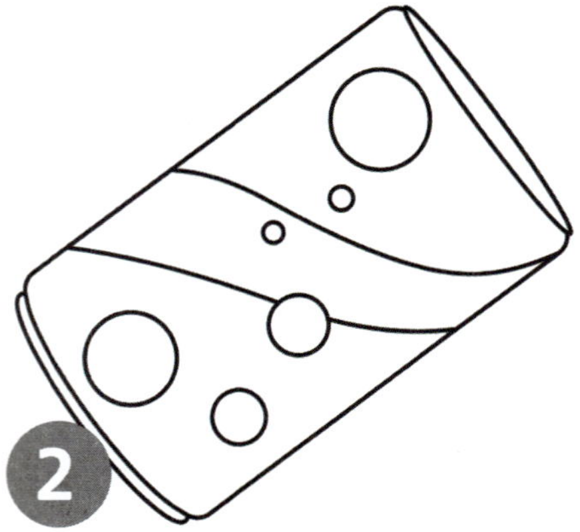
soda can

3

newspaper

4

spoon

5

jar

6

glass bottle

Key Vocabulary: *cardboard box, soda can, newspaper, spoon, jar, glass bottle*

Track: 46

Is it natural or is it human-made?

Look. Say.

Key Vocabulary: *soda can, sun, cloud, newspaper, frog, rock, cardboard box, book, plastic bottle, butterfly, glass bottle, tree, flower*

Key Language: *What is it? It's a (soda can). Is it natural or human-made? I think it's (natural).*

Can you add with a number line?

Count. Say. Write.

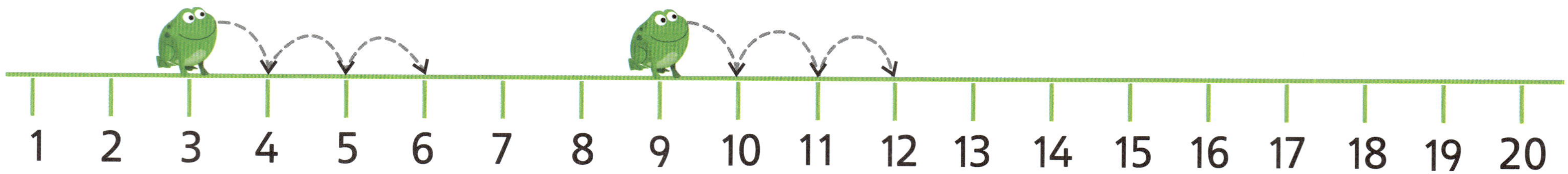

$3 + 3 = \square$ $9 + 3 = \square$

$5 + 3 = \square$ $10 + 4 = \square$

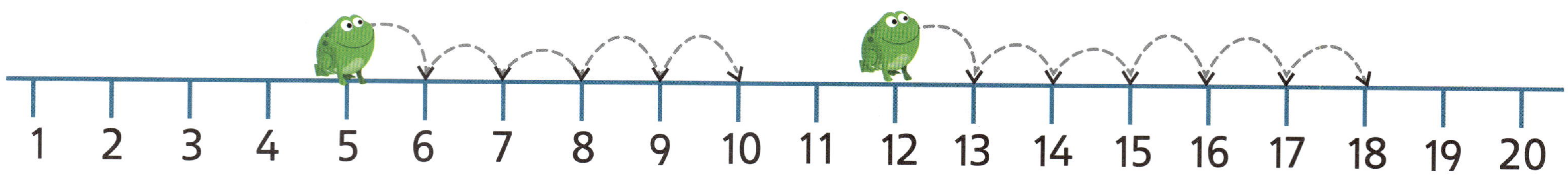

$5 + 5 = \square$ $12 + 6 = \square$

Key Vocabulary: *add, plus, equals, number line, numbers 1–20*

Key Language: *Add with a number line. (Three) plus (three) equals (six).*

Does this help the Earth?

Color. Listen. Trace.

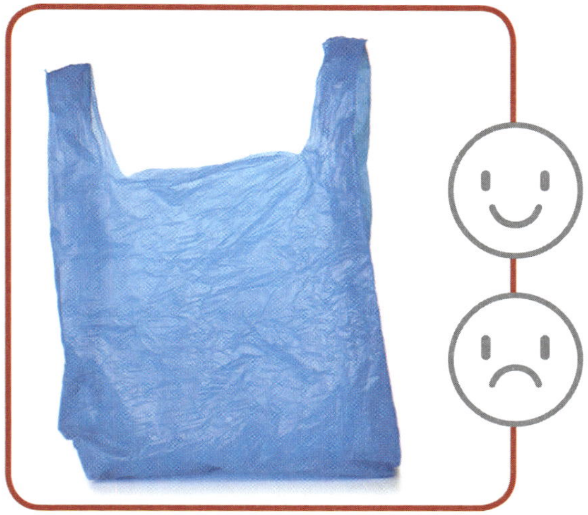

plastic bag

cloth bag

recycle

trash

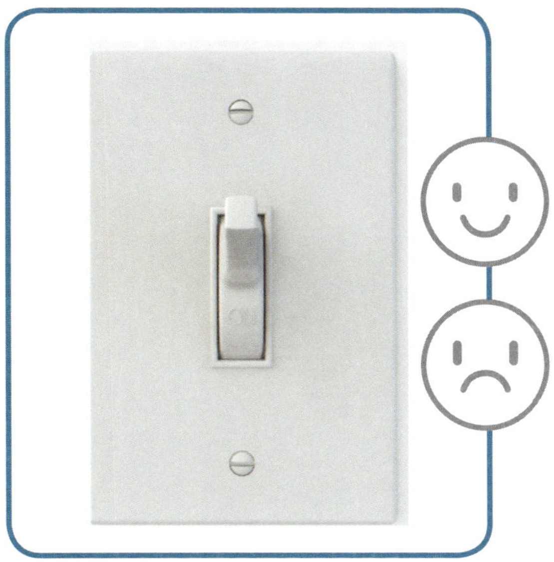

turn on

turn off

Key Vocabulary: *plastic bag, cloth bag, recycle, trash, turn on, turn off*

Key Language: *Does this help the Earth? Yes, it does. No, it doesn't. Should we (use plastic bags)?*

Track: 47

What can you do to help the Earth?

Say. Stick. Trace.

I can recycle ________.

I can use ________.

I can recycle ________.

I can turn off ________.

Key Vocabulary: *lights, cloth bag, cardboard box, soda can, bottle*

Key Language: *What can you do to help the Earth? I can (turn off the lights).*

What do you think?

Listen. Circle. Say.

What do you think about bees?

beautiful ugly

What do you think about frogs?

boring interesting

What do you think about pollution?

terrible great

What do you think about flowers?

bad important

Key Vocabulary: *pollution, bee, frog, flower, beautiful, ugly, boring, interesting, terrible, great, bad, important*

Key Language: *What do you think about (bees)? I think (bees) are (beautiful). I think (pollution) is (terrible).*

Track: 48

What can we recycle?

Say. Color. Talk.

Key

 plastic = 

 glass = 

 paper = 

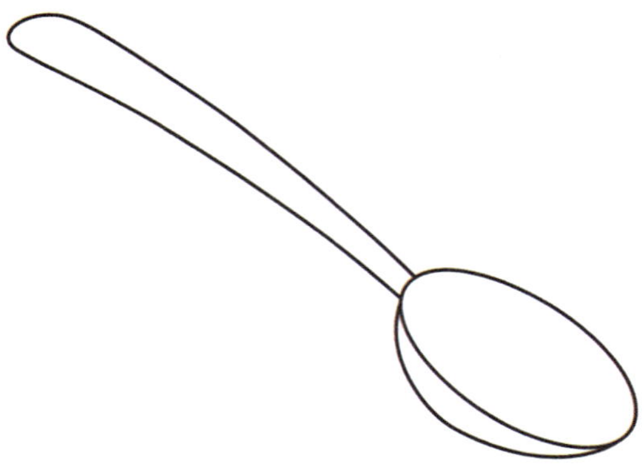

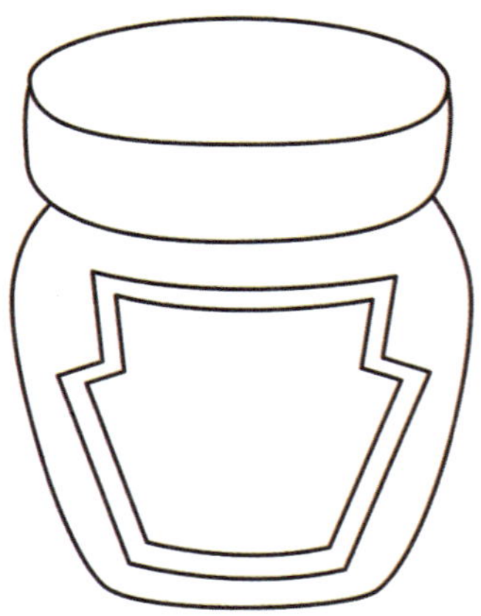

Key Vocabulary: *recycle, glass, plastic, paper*

Key Language: *Can we recycle this? What's it made of? It's made of (glass).*

How many flowers can you see?

Trace. Count. Draw.

90

Key Vocabulary: *ten, twenty, thirty, forty, fifty, sixty, seventy, eighty, ninety*

Key Language: *How many (flowers) can you see? Let's count by tens. Sets of ten. Nine sets of ten.*

Look. Make. Say.

How can we care for the Earth?

1

2

Key Vocabulary: *natural, human-made, frog, rock, paper, plastic bottle, cardboard box, soda can, newspaper, straw, plastic bag, cloth bag, recycle, trash, turn on, turn off*

Key Language: *Is it natural or human-made? What can you do to help the Earth? I can recycle newspaper. I can turn off the lights. I can save water. Can we recycle this?*

3

4

9 What do we do on vacation?

Listen. Say. Sing.

Key Vocabulary: *each, mountains, forest, amusement park, lake, summer camp*

Tracks: 49 and 50

What is the story about?

Listen. Say. Point.

Percy's Peak

Sharon

Charlie

This is Sharon, and this is Charlie.
They love going to the mountains
on vacation.

Sharon and Charlie want to get to the top
of Percy's Peak.
It's a long walk, but they feel very excited.

Key Vocabulary: *Sharon, Charlie, shine, cheese, top, long, up, down, around, excited, sad, tired*

Key Language: *What can you see? Who are the characters? What are they doing? How do they feel?*

Track: 51

How does the story help us answer our Big Question?

Listen. Point. Say.

Sharon and Charlie can't find Percy's Peak.
They sit down to rest. They feel sad and tired.

The children stand at the top of the mountain, and they look around.
The sun shines bright. What a beautiful sight!

shine

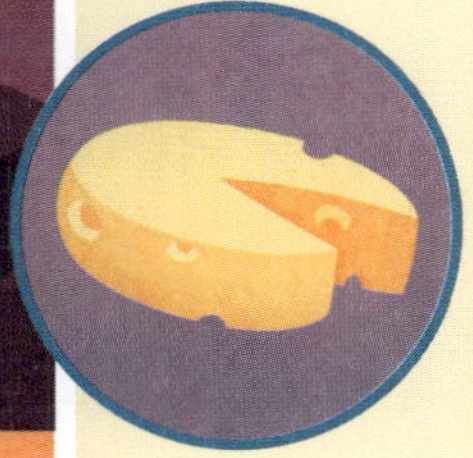

cheese

Key Vocabulary: *Sharon, Charlie, shine, cheese, top, long, up, down, around, excited, sad, tired*

Key Language: *What happens (first)? What happens at the end? Let's go up! Let's go down!*

Track: 51

Can you put the story in order?

Look. Say. Write.

Key Vocabulary: *Sharon, Charlie, shine, cheese, top, long, up, down, around, excited, sad, tired*

Key Language: *Let's put the story in order. What happens (first)? What happens at the end?*

Is it important to pick up our trash?

Draw. Trace. Talk.

Pick up your trash.

Key Vocabulary: *trash, pick up, trash can, forest, river, beach, nature*

Key Language: *Pick up our trash. Don't litter. Take care of nature.*

What are Leo and Mia missing?

Stick. Listen. Trace.

towel

flashlight

sleeping bag

sunglasses

cap

backpack

Key Vocabulary: *towel, flashlight, sleeping bag, sunglasses, cap, backpack*

Key Language: *Where's (Leo)? (He's at the beach.) What's (he) missing?*

Track: 52

What do you take to the beach?

Look. Follow. Say.

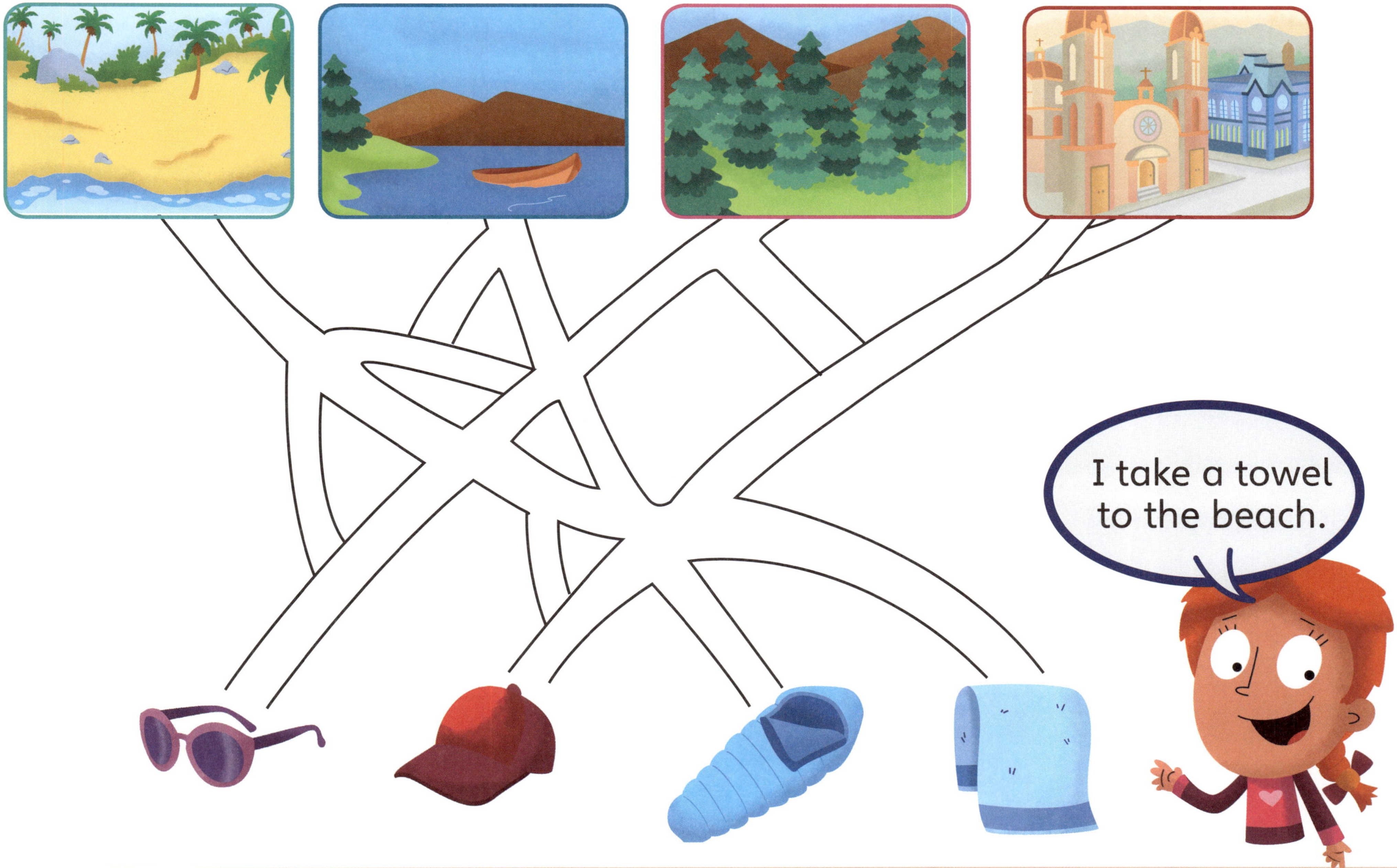

Key Vocabulary: *sunglasses, cap, sleeping bag, towel, beach, lake, forest, city*

Key Language: *What do you take to the (beach)? I take (a towel) to the (beach).*

Can you subtract with a number line?

Count. Say. Write.

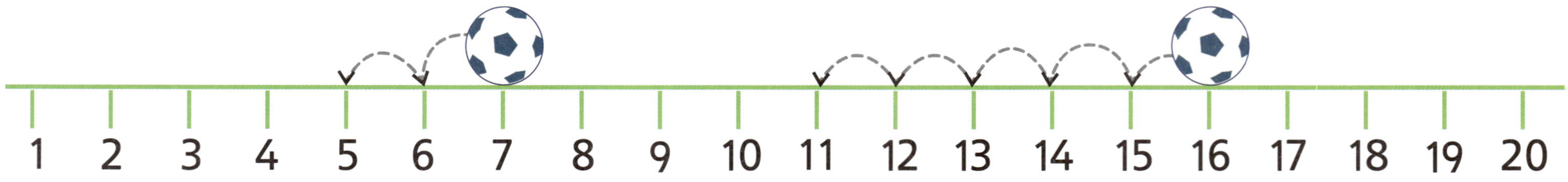

7 – 2 = ☐ 16 – 5 = ☐

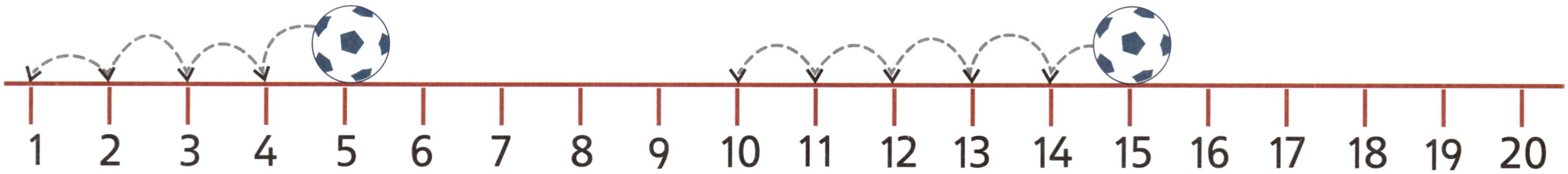

5 – 4 = ☐ 15 – 5 = ☐

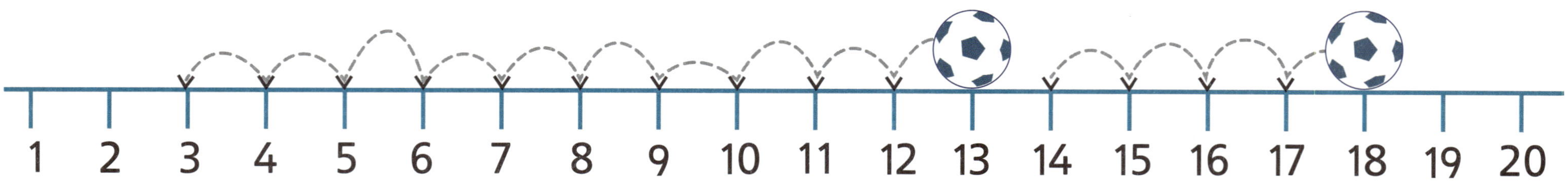

13 – 10 = ☐ 18 – 4 = ☐

Key Vocabulary: *subtract, minus, equals, number line, numbers 1–20*

Key Language: *Subtract with a number line. (Seven) minus (two) equals (five).*

What can you do on vacation?

Color. Listen. Trace.

build a sandcastle

hike

make a campfire

go on rides

row a boat

ride a horse

Key Vocabulary: *build a sandcastle, hike, make a campfire, row a boat, ride a horse, go on rides*

Key Language: *What do you do (at the lake)? I (hike).*

Track: 53

What do they do?

Look. Circle. Draw.

Key Vocabulary: *build a sandcastle, hike, make a campfire, row a boat, ride a horse, go on rides*

Key Language: *What does she do (in the mountains)? She (hikes). What do you do (in the mountains)? I (ride a horse).*

Where are you going on vacation?

Listen. Circle. Say.

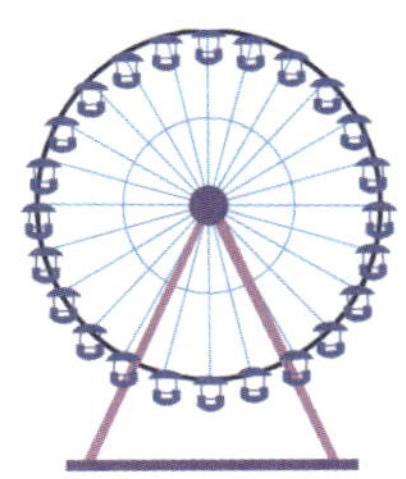

Key Vocabulary: *places, summer activities*

Key Language: *Where are you going on vacation? I'm going to the (beach). What are you going to do (at the beach)? I'm going to (build a sandcastle).*

Track: 54

What can we do on vacation at night?

Draw. Paint. Say.

I can ______________________________.

Key Vocabulary: *places, summer activities*

Key Language: *What can you do on vacation at night? I can (make a campfire).*

How many suns can you see?

Trace. Count. Draw.

100

Key Vocabulary: *ten, twenty, thirty, forty, fifty, sixty, seventy, eighty, ninety, one hundred*

Key Language: *How many (suns) can you see? Let's count by tens. Sets of ten. Ten sets of ten.*

Look. Make. Say.

What do we do on vacation?

1

2

3

4

Key Vocabulary: *beach, mountains, forest, amusement park, lake, summer camp, cap, towel, sunglasses, sleeping bag, backpack, flashlight, build a sandcastle, hike, make a campfire, go on rides, row a boat, ride a horse, pick up our trash, don't litter, take care of nature*

Key Language: *What do you take to the (beach)? I take a (towel) to the (beach). What do you do (in the mountains)? I (hike), Where are you going on vacation? I'm going to the (mountains). What are you going to do? I'm going to (make a campfire).*

Name Tree

Cut. Trace. Glue.

Ask: *What happens to the leaves in fall?* Provide any necessary language. Help children write a letter of their name in each leaf. Then children trace over each letter of their name. Children cut out the letters and glue them in the correct order to write their name. Finally, children attach their name trees to a bulletin board.

Winter Game

Cut. Play.

Name each of the items: *snowman, snowflake, gloves, scarf, boots, skates, sled, hot cocoa.* Children repeat each word. Divide the class into pairs. Children cut out the cards and play Memory.

Spring Wreath

Cut. Paint. Glue.

Ask: *What's the weather like in spring?* Provide any necessary language. Help children cut out a wreath from a paper plate and paint it green. Then they cut out the pictures and glue them onto their wreath. Finally, attach a string on the top of the wreath to hang it.

Summer Sunglasses

Cut. Glue. Make.

Ask: *What's the weather like in summer?* Provide any necessary language. Children color in the sunglasses. Then they cut out the sunglasses and glue them onto construction paper. Finally, cut out the sunglasses again and put them on. Provide assistance as needed.

Unit 1, p. 10

Unit 2, p. 24

Unit 3, p. 42

Unit 4, p. 51

Unit 5, p. 65

Unit 6, p. 81

Unit 7, p. 93

Unit 8, p. 110

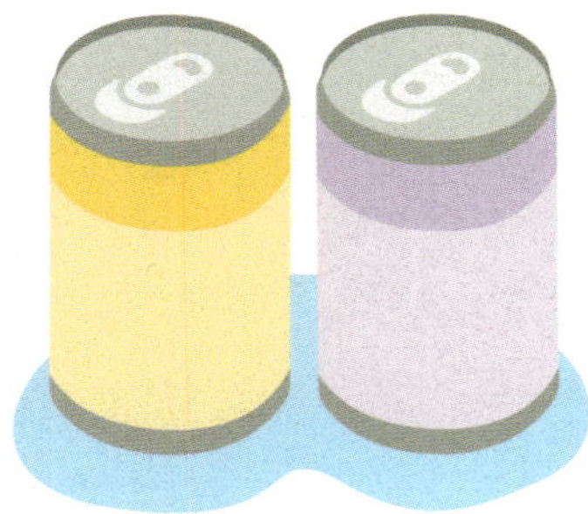

Unit 9, p. 120